Better Together

how the animals we love
can inspire our creativity and
transform our shared lives

Christine King

Credits

Cover image: Huge thanks to TeamJackson (@ iStock.com by Getty Images) for this gorgeous photo!

Printing and distribution: Kindle Direct Publishing (kdp.amazon..com)

Published by **Anima** Books
a division of **Anima** Vet
Emerald, Victoria
Australia
animabooks.com.au

ISBN: 979-8-8669-5805-4 (hardcover)
ISBN: 979-8-8669-5842-9 (paperback)

Dedication

For Miss Lilly, my furry soul friend.

Contents

Acknowledgements

Those familiar with the work of Sanaya Roman *(Living with Joy)* and of Esther and Jerry Hicks *(The Law of Attraction, Ask and It Is Given)* will recognize some of the 'Orin' and 'Abraham' teachings in this book. These and many other authors have inspired me and guided my thinking over the years.

In no particular order, they also include Candace Pert, PhD *(Molecules of Emotion, Everything You Need to Know to Feel Go(o)d)*, Bruce Lipton, PhD *(The Biology of Belief)*, Gregg Braden *(Secrets of the Lost Mode of Prayer)*, Pema Chodron *(When Things Fall Apart)*, Alan Watts *(This is It, The Joyous Cosmology)*, Neil Douglas-Klotz *(Prayers of the Cosmos, The Hidden Gospel)*, the many poems of Rumi, and Ursula Le Guin's beautiful translation of *The Tao te Ching*.

You see, the concepts I discuss in this book are as old as the hills. They just haven't been the predominant 'rules of the game' we humans have been playing. But as Victor Hugo observed:

> *"Greater than the tread of mighty armies*
> *is an idea whose time has come."*

My heartfelt thanks to each and every one of these authors, and to all of the other teachers who have guided me over the years, only some of whom are human.

Prologue

I wasn't looking for a dog. I wasn't in the right place in my life; I wasn't settled enough, and a dog would have further disrupted my rather unmoored life. What I most wanted was to settle somewhere and put down roots. But where? And doing what?

Wandering had never suited me. I hated change, yet I could never settle to anything for very long. I would inevitably outgrow what I thought I'd most wanted and where I'd most wanted to be. 'Wanderlust' was a foreign concept to me — a character flaw, in fact. Yet wandering was what I found myself doing for what ended up stretching into decades. So, at the time, I didn't want to commit to as much as a house plant!

I first met Tiger Lilly in the summer of 2002, when I was visiting my friend Linda. She and her husband had a lovely little farm on the outskirts of Chapel Hill, North Carolina, surrounded by woods and fields. I was there late one afternoon to do some bodywork on her horse. It was early evening when I was finishing up and getting ready to leave. As Linda and I stood chatting in the doorway of the barn, her neighbor Brenda came over with a skinny, flea-infested, brindle (tiger-striped) dog on the end of a piece of old rope.

The dog was a young bitch who'd evidently just weaned a litter of puppies, because a pendulous udder hung down beneath her toast-rack of a body. Brenda asked if Linda knew the dog, who'd turned up a little while earlier. No, Linda had never seen the dog before and had no idea where she might have come from. Kind soul that she is, Linda offered to post some flyers around the neighborhood if Brenda would take care of the dog until someone claimed her or they found her a new home.

The dog was quite an odd-looking creature. Imagine what would happen if you crossed a Greyhound with a Staffie (Staffordshire bull terrier)... That was Tiger Lilly, who later came to be known simply as Miss Lilly. (Her full name was The Splendid Miss Tiger Lilly. Good name for a drag queen, right? ☺) Being brindle, there was only a handful of things she could have been; but other than her striped coat, she didn't look like any of them.

Rural North Carolina is notorious for getting... shall we say, "creative" with dog breeding, so I never did get any closer to unlocking the mysteries of her heritage — and as dog-fighting was as popular there as hunting, I didn't even want to know! Instead, I variously called her a Carolina Truck Hound (sounds official, but I made that one up), my Stripey Dog, or a Bitza (that's Aussie slang for a mixed-breed dog, one that's made up of "bitza this and bitza that"; also known as the Heinz 57).

The poor thing was covered in fleas and ticks, and she looked like she hadn't had a good meal in months. Her teeth showed her to be a young dog, and her subsequent development put her at about 12–18 months of age at the time. What stood out to me most, though, was her sweet temperament. She was lovely! As I later got to know her, I came to realize just how stressed she'd been when we first met. Still, she was obliging as I looked her over and examined her teeth, and as we humans stood around talking about what to do with her.

As I said, I didn't want a dog at the time. I was an Australian veterinarian, living in the United States for the time being. I'd moved to the US in 1993 to do a large-animal internal medicine residency at North Carolina State University's College of Veterinary Medicine. It was a two-year program and the plan was to complete the residency, sit the American College of Veterinary Internal Medicine board exams, and then return home to Australia as a specialist in equine internal medicine. But life had other plans, and 9 years later I was still there.

Whenever anyone asked what had brought me to the US and what was keeping me there, I would always answer the latter by shrugging and adding,

"I don't know. I just know that this is the place for me to be right now; and when that changes, I'll move."

To me, it was as clear as day that I was in the right place; but for what reason, I didn't know. It never seemed all that important for me to know *why*. It was enough to know that *there* was where I was supposed to be for now.

As the two neighbors had a plan, I drove home, confident that the dog was in good hands. But as the days went by, I couldn't stop thinking about her. Unbidden, that stripey dog would pop into my mind at odd times through the day, and I'd wonder where she was now and who was looking after her. When I went back to Linda's place the following week, I asked her what had happened with the dog.

"Oh, I'm so upset about that!" she said. "Brenda had Animal Control come and take the dog away."

Brenda had been keeping her outside, but the dog wanted to be in the house, and in an effort to get Brenda to let her in, she'd accidentally torn a small hole in the screen door with her nails. Later, I came to know this scratching at the door as a sign that Miss Lilly was very anxious and needed to be inside, where she felt safe. Perhaps there'd been a storm coming; she was always very anxious during thunderstorms. Anyway, without mentioning it to Linda, Brenda had simply had the dog picked up by Animal Control and taken to an animal shelter.

I fretted about that for days. No matter how hard I tried, I couldn't get the dog off my mind. She was such a strange-looking thing! I wish I had a dollar for every time we were out on a walk and a stranger said to me,

"Is that a hyena?"

"Yes," I wanted to reply matter-of-factly, "I have a hyena."

I'm pretty sure they were mixing up their African animals, because she looked more like the Cape hunting dog, also known as the African wild dog. As she was no longer a puppy, I was sure she'd be euthanized because no-one would want her, and the county animal shelters are always full to overflowing and running on shoe-string budgets.

But still I resisted adopting her. I had a 'green card' (US permanent residency status), but I had no firm plans to stay in the US indefinitely. I loved living there, yet I expected that I would return to Australia at some point. Adopting a dog would anchor me in the US for the duration of her life, as I would not put a dog through the 6-months-long rabies quarantine that Australia required for dogs and cats arriving from the US at the time, not to mention the long flight in the cargo hold.

I also had the recurring thought that if I adopted her, I'd simply be signing up to have my heart broken at some point. Perhaps it's an occupational hazard, but it's long been clear to me that, in sharing our lives with animals as companions, we're signing up for a master class on love and loss. Unless we die unexpectedly or we adopt a puppy when we're in our nineties, we are almost certainly going to outlive our animal companions. (Of course, there are other exceptions, including long-lived species such as cockatoos and tortoises.)

In other words, we are almost certainly going to have our hearts broken. And I did — but broken wide open, and in the most unexpected ways.

Over the years, I've often thought about that much-quoted line from Tennyson's poem, *In Memoriam*, which he wrote as a requiem for a beloved friend:

"Tis better to have loved and lost than never to have loved at all."

I'd always hated that line! To me, the prospect of love had never seemed worth the inevitable pain of loss. Put another way, the prospect of loss seemed far worse than missing out on anything that love might offer. I'd rather avoid loss than risk love. But Miss Lilly wormed her way into my heart and changed my mind about all that. Now I just shake my head in wonder at all I very nearly missed out on, simply because I feared the loss that would undoubtedly ensue at some point.

I remember very clearly the moment I realized she was mine: I was driving along the interstate, thinking about nothing in particular, when the thought, "Tiger Lilly; her name is Tiger Lilly," popped into my mind. Oh, no! I'd named her. There was no hope for me now!

As soon as I got home, I called Linda, tracked down my Tiger Lilly to the animal shelter where she'd been taken — the last of three possible county shelters where she might have been held — and went to get her. There I stood at the counter, pleading with the careworn receptionist not to make me go back and look through the kennels for the dog I could so accurately describe to her.

"*Please* don't make me go look at the dogs," I begged, "I'll go home with twenty!"

Her eyebrows lifted and a hopeful smile flashed briefly across her face before she relented and kindly began leafing through the enormous folder of current inmates. There was only one dog who matched the description I gave her, and after what felt like an interminable wait in the tiny visiting room, Tiger Lilly finally arrived.

She was as sweet as I remembered, but she showed no particular interest in me, being so anxious to be out of that awful place. I later became very familiar with that worried expression, the tension in her body, and the mental shutting down as she blocked out everything but her avenue of escape from the situation she found so distressing. Still, I knew she was mine, so after signing the adoption papers and fitting her new harness, we headed for home.

Thus began the most profound and wonderful relationship of my life so far. Miss Lilly did indeed anchor me in the US, for the next fifteen years. In fact, she served as an anchor through the most turbulent and transformative period of my life, which included a long struggle with recurring bouts of severe depression and repeated thoughts of suicide.

Miss Lilly saved my life many times over. I can say with certainty, because I well remember the decision-making process, that I would have been long dead right now if not for her. When I adopted her, I made a commitment to take good care of her for the rest of her life and to make her life as good as it could be. I would not go back on my word to her, no matter how hard it was at times to go on.

The idea for this book arose from some meditations and musings on the role Miss Lilly had played in my life. Yes, she kept me alive through some very dark times. But she also made my life *better* in the process. Although she's been gone for almost 7 years now, she's still teaching me as I've pondered the ways in which these special animals come into our lives and, together, we make each other's life better.

Initially, I titled the book *Soul Friends,* because I now think of Miss Lilly as my soul friend. I have never doubted that if humans have souls, then animals do, too, even when it flew in the face of my conservative Christian upbringing.

It just never seemed right — neither fair nor true — that animals wouldn't get to go to the heaven I believed in at the time. Since then, my spiritual journey has taken me on a very wild ride, from the fundamentalist Christianity of my childhood (Seventh-Day Adventist) through atheism, Taoism, Buddhism, and various New Age philosophies, to a rather bleak materialism, and finally to a cosmology of my own that has (and needs) no name.

Perhaps it's a view I'll come to revise in time, but during one meditation an image popped into my mind of Miss Lilly as a dog-shaped extension of my own ... what shall I call it, the vastly greater, nonphysical part of our being ... *soul,* for want of a better term, one that is less burdened by religiosity.

I perceive that greater, nonphysical part of my being as a gorgeous sphere of irrepressibly lively, iridescent 'stuff' which extends into the physical world as a me-shaped human form, a human-shaped extension of this formative ... *stuff.* Over to the right of me was the outline of Miss Lilly, a dog-shaped form extending into the world from the same stuff.

Although this is a very dull analogy for such a scintillating mental image, it reminded me a bit of Claymation (clay animation) figures, such as the animated television series for children in which each figure arises from the base of clay, has its adventure (usually with other figures who are doing the same), and then disappears back into the base of clay when it's done.

Perhaps a better analogy is ocean waves that arise and then settle back into the sea. Many years ago, I was looking out the window of an airplane as we were coming in to land at a coastal airport. From that perspective, the white caps of the individual waves near the shore would appear and then disappear as each wave formed and then dissolved back into the sea. It was a long time ago, but I distinctly remember thinking that it was a good metaphor for a life.

So, this book began from the realization that Miss Lilly and I shared the same source, the same formative stuff, and *that* made her my soul friend, who manifested for a time as an odd-looking, stripey dog named Tiger Lilly.

But after some reflection, I changed the title to *Better Together*. Not only has the term 'soul friend' become rather cliché, but I wanted to write a book that could be embraced even by those with no spiritual inclination or who, like me, have unpleasant memories of a religious upbringing that can only be described as repressive.

While this book would appear to be about me and Miss Lilly, it is really for you and the animals you love. I hope you'll see something of yourself and *your* precious ones on every page, and that all of our lives are made better in return.

Chapter 1

Drawn together

When I was 3 or 4 years old, as the family chronicles go, we were driving home from somewhere or other when we passed a dead goanna on the side of the road. (If you're unfamiliar with goannas, they're large, carnivorous lizards that are native to Australia. They're known elsewhere as monitor lizards.) 'Dead' doesn't mean anything to a small child, of course, so according to my dad I badgered him all the way home about the goanna, asking questions such as "What happened to him? Why is he dead? Who made him dead? Will he be alright? Where's his mummy? But who's going to take care of him?"

I don't remember that particular incident, but I also can't recall a time when I didn't love animals. They're absolutely magical to me, and I'm utterly fascinated by them. I love the character of Newt Scamander, the "magizoologist" JK Rowling created for the Harry Potter prequel *Fantastic Beasts and Where to Find Them*. He's never met a creature he didn't love, and he feels more comfortable around animals and connects better with them than with people. She's onto something there!

It's a simple fact that we animal lovers are drawn to animals in a way that others don't understand and we can't explain very well. Nor do we feel any particular need to explain. It's just the way we're made, and we wonder what on earth is wrong with people who don't like animals!

It's as if animals have a tractor beam that draws us inexorably to them. We may be moved — our mood brightened, our heart lifted, our mind expanded — by spending time in nature or by music, art, dancing, surfing, gardening, cooking, … any number of things; but animals hold a special place in our hearts and thus in our lives.

> We animal lovers are drawn to animals,
> and they hold a special place in our lives.

Perhaps it's simply that animals, being sentient and expressive in ways we recognize as similar to our own, respond in ways we find meaningful. If so, then we're attributing meaning simply to please ourselves, which is one definition of anthropomorphism (attributing human thoughts, emotions, and motivations to other species), a mortal sin in science.

But that explanation reduces us to cravenly transactional creatures, where we only love animals as long as they (seem to) love us in return. That's certainly true of some people, but assuredly not all. No; in my experience, there's vastly more to it — and to *us* — than that.

Furthermore, that explanation utterly fails to account for a phenomenon that interests me greatly and which is a through-line in this book: While we love and care about animals in general, and we may have a decided preference for one species and even one breed, we are inexplicably drawn to certain *individuals* in particular, and we form deep and lasting connections with these special ones.

Often, the connection is instantaneous, such as when a certain puppy or kitten in a litter is so clearly the one for us. Other times, the bond develops gradually. I suspect that what makes the difference is how open we are at the time. That was certainly the case with me and Miss Lilly. It took me a while to "get with the program" and to care for her so deeply. It took me much, much longer to understand the true nature and value of our friendship.

We are inexplicably drawn to certain *individuals,* and we form deep and lasting connections.

The human–animal bond has been the subject of extensive study and discussion, both in the scientific literature and in books for those of us who share our lives with animals. The explanations for this particular phenomenon vary widely, from "opposites attract" (*e.g.,* a bold person adopts the really shy kitten) to *its* opposite, "birds of a feather" or mirroring, where we see something of ourselves in the animal (*e.g.,* a shy person adopts the really shy kitten).

None of the explanations put forward are universally true, probably because the reasons for individual human–animal bonds are as complex and nuanced as the people and animals themselves. In other words, each human–animal bond is as unique as the human and animal involved.

Furthermore, I don't think it *can* be distilled down to a set of psychological or behavioral principles. In my experience, both personal and professional, there's more to it than that — because there's more to each of *us* than that.

I used to think that there was something wrong with me because I cared more for my dog than I do for most people. But the fact is that my friendship with Miss Lilly was the single most profound relationship of my life thus far. I love my family and my friends; I love my dog more.

> For some of us, these friendships are the
> most profound relationships of our life.

Even though she's long gone, I still use the present tense for the love I have for her, because it has not died; it has not even dimmed. Such is the nature of love. Miss Lilly was able to get through to me in a way that other people had not, that other people *could* not at the time.

I've since heard similar sentiments expressed about their animals by other people:

"He was the love of my life."

"I've never loved a living creature more than I loved him."

"My husband and I both agree that we loved our dog more than we love each other."

That last one was a bit of a stunner, as it was said by someone in a long and apparently happy marriage. And whenever I mentioned this book to animal lovers as I was writing it, their faces would light up, and some even teared up, as they proceeded to tell me about *their* special animals. Such is the depth of feeling these beautiful creatures can inspire in us.

It is now my view that we are palpably drawn together because we are meant to find one another and be part of each other's life as mutual friends, helpers, guardians, and guides. In this regard, our animal soul friends are no different from our human soul friends — our *Anam Cara,* as Irish theologian John O'Donohue labelled these precious friendships.

> We are palpably drawn together because
> we are meant to find one another.

In my experience, these special animals come into our lives at a time and in a way that is significant and unique to each of us. So, too, their departure. Everything in between is likewise significant and unique to us. Each of our stories is different, but one thing is common to all:

> These special animals come into our lives
> and change *everything.*

Most of all, they change *us...*

***

Chapter 2

Better together

We'd love them anyway, because that's our nature. But there's a distinct advantage to having these special animals in our lives: they make our lives more interesting, more fun, more rich, and vastly more satisfying.

In short, our lives are *better* together.

The way I understand it now, the key element is this: Loving them, and being loved in return, makes us *feel good;* and *that* changes *everything.*

I had no idea of the tremendous power of this effect at the time, but I *was* dimly aware that Miss Lilly wasn't just company in my otherwise solitary life. Nor was she much of a protector. She'd happily have let almost anyone into the house with a welcoming smile and a wagging tail. She did look rather fearsome, so to anyone who didn't know or like dogs, her mere presence in our yard or on our walks was a deterrent; but that was all a façade. She was a dog who seldom met a person she didn't like. (And when she didn't like someone, I knew to take note.)

I often called Miss Lilly my dog fairy because she seemed so other-worldly to me, when in reality she was simply much more light and carefree than me. (My sister suggested that perhaps I should call Miss Lilly my fairy dogmother. ☺)

Miss Lilly had a great smile, and she smiled often. One of the reasons I think she had a heaping helping of Staffie in her background was because her whole head would crack open in a gigantic grin, what I think of as the Staffie smile.

I wish dogs had a laugh that human ears could hear, because I think she loved to laugh. Miss Lilly was a dog who exuded joy and a great sense of fun when she felt safe and secure. Those are qualities I inherited in spades from my dad but that I'd steadily lost along the way through childhood into adulthood, and particularly in my professional life. Life just wasn't fun anymore — until Miss Lilly came along.

> Life just wasn't fun anymore
> — until Miss Lilly came along.

Of all our many shared moments over the fifteen years we lived together, one stands out in my mind as epitomizing her great sense of fun and adventure: Miss Lilly standing with her nose practically touching the floor-to-ceiling, plate-glass window of a 24th-floor apartment and smiling with surprise and glee as a seagull flew right by her nose.

She looked back at me with a big grin, as if to say, "Isn't this great!" I'm afraid of heights, so I couldn't go anywhere near that wall of windows! She, on the other hand, thought it was just wonderful!

We'd recently moved from Cary, North Carolina to Seattle, Washington and I hadn't yet found us a place to live. The friends we'd been staying with arranged for us to use their friend's empty apartment for a couple of weeks while I continued the search. It was in a high-rise building in downtown Seattle that looked out over Puget Sound.

What a surreal experience: navigating all those one-way streets and all that traffic, parking underground, going up and down in the elevator just to take Miss Lilly outside for a pee, having to walk two blocks to find the nearest grass… (OK, I can hear the urbanites sniggering from here, but for us country girls it was quite the experience!)

> To her, it was a grand adventure,
> and the windows were Dog TV.

And then there was that wall of glass. Yikes! But Miss Lilly wasn't fazed by any of it. To her, it was a grand adventure, and the windows were Dog TV. She was absolutely delighted by the seagulls flying around right outside her window. She also loved to look down and watch all the cars on Alaskan Way, the road that runs along the waterfront, right below us. It must have been like watching an ant farm! Goodness; it makes me dizzy just thinking about it…

No doubt, it's a pet dog's privilege not to be worried about where to live, how to make a living, and all the other common anxieties of human life. But one could argue that those anxieties were mine precisely *because* I worried about them. Certainly, the practicalities of life deserve my attention, but worrying has never done me any good.

And yet worrying had become a deeply ingrained habit. All too often, I'd be spun off to someplace else in my mind, chewing over the past or fretting about some imagined calamity in the future. My thoughts would churn over the mistakes I'd made (both real and imagined), when I wasn't getting all worked up about the things I feared might happen next. Very little of my attention was trained on enjoying the present moment, on experiencing *The Power of Now,* as author Eckhart Tolle would say.

Just by being there, Miss Lilly served as a reminder to focus my attention on the here-and-now, and to notice and enjoy the many and varied delights life brings us, even in the midst of massive upheaval.

> Miss Lilly reminded me to notice and enjoy the many and varied delights life brings us.

But I didn't yet know how much that state of mind would have helped me in making the thousand decisions involved in moving across the country, finding us a place to live, and then starting a veterinary practice from scratch (something I discuss in Chapter 4).

More than anything else, spending time with Miss Lilly, in *her* world rather than mine, made me *feel good.* Looking back, that was perhaps her greatest gift to me, her most important role in my life. She made my life better because when I felt good, I made better decisions.

Here, I want to pause and acknowledge again some of my favorite authors for helping me see the practical importance, the real *value*, of feeling good — because I haven't always trusted that feeling. In fact, I'd long ago gotten into the habit of pinching it off before it really had a chance to take hold.

For one thing, I didn't want to be accused of being "unprofessional" (another scientific mortal sin) or of being a "Pollyanna." In vet school, I had a classmate who always seemed to be smiling and upbeat. The running joke was that, if told the world would be ending that night, Cathy would be heard saying, "Well, 'bye everyone; see you in the morning!"

But even more than avoiding criticism or ridicule, I wanted to avoid being disappointed when the good feeling inevitably faded and left me feeling worse than if I'd never had it at all, like being cast out of paradise.

> Miss Lilly made my life better because
> when I felt good, I made better decisions.

I've since learned to *appreciate* these good feelings, to *revel* in them, and to *use* them when I have decisions to make, big or small, because what I now know is this:

When I feel good, I'm more creative and confident, inspired and intrepid.

When I feel good, I trust life — and myself — more.

When I feel good, I know what to do, and I know that it will turn out well, even when the process takes me via "the scenic route." (More on that in a bit.)

When I feel good, I know when to act. Just as importantly, I know when to wait.

When I feel good, waiting is fine; waiting is even an enjoyable state as I eagerly anticipate what it is I'm waiting for.

When I feel good, I revel in the unfolding of my creations, of the things I'm inspired to create. I enjoy the process, including the pace and manner in which it unfolds, the course it takes.

When I feel good, my health improves, along with my sense of well-being.

> When I feel good, I'm filled with
> love and clarity, peace and power.

When I feel good, I'm more kind and compassionate.

When I feel good, I'm a better writer, veterinarian, partner, neighbor, daughter, sister, friend, colleague, customer… *All* of my relationships, with others *and* myself, improve.

In short, when I feel good, I'm filled with love and clarity, peace and power.

Of course, the *opposite* happens when I *don't* feel good. I know I'm not alone here; for many of us, that's an all-too-familiar state. We don't make good decisions in that state.

When I *don't* feel good, I may be timid or indecisive; and when I *do* decide, I do so out of fear, from a sense of lack or limitation. Or I push ahead, forcing things, when it would have been better to wait.

When I *don't* feel good, I often become impatient, frustrated, and even angry when the thing I want doesn't materialize when and how I think it should. I'm quick to lose faith in my vision *and* myself, in my ability to create the life I want.

When I *don't* feel good, I act from an imagined sense that all I can expect or hope to achieve is only what someone like me has achieved, and no more; perhaps not even that much. Oh, I may fantasize about more for myself, but I don't really believe I can have it, or I might get it only after years of struggle and hard work, and a great deal of luck.

When I *don't* feel good, I imagine a much smaller and far more difficult life for myself.

In short, when I *don't* feel good, I imagine a much smaller and far more difficult life for myself.

I've thought a lot about why I've spent so much time in that state of mind, controlled by that set of beliefs about life. I came to the realization that I'd absorbed without question the prevailing "wisdom" of our time: that life has its ups and downs, so we just have to take things as they come; and that success takes a lot of time, effort, and luck.

"Plan for the worst, hope for the best, and accept whatever comes" is a common axiom, and one I first heard from my atheist father — to the great consternation of my Christian mother, because to her it completely discounted God.

But Mum's God, the one I was taught to believe in as a child, appeared to be just as capricious, unpredictably meting out reward and punishment in a cryptical "Father knows best" sort of way, where painful things are "all part of God's plan" and, if not punishment for some unwitting sin, deliberately designed to be "for our own good" and "never more than we can bear." (Oh, dear; my roots are showing! ☺)

Whether secular or religious, these and similar sentiments reinforce the belief that life is largely something that *happens* to us, whether by accident, chance, luck, fate, or divine will; that we have very little control over our lives, and whatever control we do have must be exerted with great effort and with the certain knowledge that the outcome is uncertain.

> Like any belief, this notion is self-fulfilling
> and thus self-perpetuating.

So, really, there isn't much difference among these various drivers of our variable experience. It all just *happens* to us, whether we like it or not; whether we want it or not.

The trouble is that, like any belief, this notion is self-fulfilling and thus self-reinforcing, trapping us in an endless bind of our own belief. Its self-perpetuation makes it the primary argument against an equally valid belief that we are indeed in control of our own experience.

But accepting the simplistic "we create our own reality" at face value gets us caught in a different kind of trap, and I've fallen into that one, too. When applied as a plaster, the pain and disillusionment it can cause is all too real.

The way I understand it now is this: what I focus on, whether I like it or not, whether I want it or not, and the beliefs I hold, whether affirming or limiting, create my *perception* of what is, because we primarily see what we *focus* on and experience what we *believe* to be true.

My habitual focus on the things I didn't want (unpleasant memories, things I don't like about the present, things I fear might happen in the future, *etc.*) and the underlying beliefs (I'm not good enough, I'm too much of this and not enough of that, life is largely something that just happens to me, *etc.*) had led to a reality that I was not enjoying very much.

> We primarily see what we *focus* on
> and experience what we *believe* to be true.

It took me a lifetime to learn that I needed to change my habitual focus to the things I *do* want, and to examine my beliefs about my worthiness or ability to have them, and drop the beliefs that were holding me back and creating a very unsatisfying reality.

Most of those beliefs weren't mine anyway. They were learned from my parents, taught to me by others (teachers, church leaders, *etc.*), or passively absorbed from society in general (I'm looking at you, advertising industry!). Those beliefs may not have *become* mine by choice, but now they *remain* mine *only* by choice.

And then there are the limiting beliefs we create ourselves. For most of my life, my earliest memory was of my mother laughing at me for making a mistake. Not surprisingly,

I hate being ridiculed and I hate making mistakes. The particular incident occurred when I was 3 or 4 years old (evidently an important time in my young life).

I can still see it clearly in my mind: Mum opening a draw under my sister's bed to find that it contained a dead mouse, lying on its side. The mouse was so long dead that it was mummified, its little limbs contracted into the characteristic boxer's stance, its tail sticking out stiffly behind it.

"A kangaroo!" I exclaimed, so pleased and proud of myself for correctly identifying this animal.

Mum laughed as she said, "*That's* not a kangaroo!" Almost 60 years on, I can still feel the sting of that scoffing remark.

> A belief may not have *become* mine by choice, but now it *remains* mine *only* by choice.

A couple of years ago, after I'd moved back home to help my sister take care of Mum in her final years, I was driving Mum home from a doctor's appointment along a road we hadn't taken before. Roadworks had sent us down a different route. Mum pointed to a side road and mentioned that we used to live down there, when I was very young. I didn't remember it at all, so she began talking about when we'd first moved in.

She'd opened a cupboard under the kitchen counter to find a dead mouse curled up on the shelf. Precocious child that I was, I'd burst forth and declared,

"*That's* not a kangaroo!"

Mum laughed, delighted by her smart little kid. Almost 60 years on, she was still delighted by the memory of her smart little kid.

It was a different house, a different part of the house, a different type of cabinet, and a different person making that declaration, for a very different reason. I'd gotten most of the elements completely wrong, and it colored my whole life until Mum, unbidden and unbeknown to her, relieved me of that painful and limiting belief I'd formed and held against myself for practically a lifetime.

Such is the power of belief and the potential that is unleashed when limiting beliefs are at last discarded.

> Great potential is unleashed
> when limiting beliefs are discarded.

As for perceived setbacks and failures — life's "downs" — that was another essential lesson I had yet to learn. We don't need to move in a straight line or at warp speed to reach our goals. In fact, what I finally realized is that taking "the scenic route," as I now think of it, was *essential* for me because it gave me the time I needed to grow into the vision I now have for my life. It also enabled me to pick up the variety of skills, experiences, perspectives, and connections I'd need in order to *reach* my new goals.

And as the mouse/kangaroo story illustrates, I've even learned to see apparent roadblocks and detours as *directions,* guiding me to a better way, a better course of action, or a better perspective on something. Missteps *should* feel difficult, they *should* feel wrong, as these uncomfortable feelings serve as warning signs. That's how we're made.

When I pay attention to these feelings and let them serve as an indicator that I'm on the wrong track, or that I'm pushing when I should be relaxing and inviting inspiration, invariably I find my way to what I really want, often down a surprising path, one I may not have considered before.

There's an invisible slipstream or flow to life that I *feel* for now because I've learned to trust it completely. It never fails to guide me to what I really want, which is not always what I thought I wanted when I set out.

> The new way, and for me the best way,
> is to focus on *receiving*.

A change in the way I thought about, and moved through, life was long overdue. The old way, which is the dominant way in our society still, emphasizes *achieving*: starting from a place of lack or want, striving to achieve, and celebrating hard-won victories over… what, Life? Adversity? Obstacles? Inertia? Unpredictability? The reluctance of Life to give up its rewards without a fight? The list is limited only by our imagination, which is deeply rooted in our beliefs.

The new way, and for me the best way — in fact, the *only* way I want to be living — is to focus on *receiving*: inspiration, specific ideas, the enthusiasm and energy to act on them, co-operative elements, synergy, and lastly the thing itself, in all its material glory. This list too is limited only by our imagination, which likewise is deeply rooted in our beliefs.

As long as I drop my well-practiced habits of worry and doubt, and I remain *sure* that I will succeed at some point, I generally do. As long as I proceed from a place of *trust* that life can deliver up whatever I need, as long as my focus and faith are unwavering, things generally turn out well.

Distraction is perhaps my biggest obstacle. It is a well-worn groove as well, no doubt because it acts as an anodyne to worry, doubt, frustration, and all the rest. The habit I've been cultivating instead, and the subject of the next chapter, is to *enjoy* myself — which is to say, to emphasize feeling good.

> The power of feeling good
> is the key to *everything*.

Although it flies in the face of pretty much everything we're taught about life, about responsibility, duty, and the virtue and necessity of hard work, I now resolve to do what I love. I trust that the feelings of enthusiasm and enjoyment are the ground on which we exist, the very essence of us. It's simply covered up much of the time, spontaneously revealing itself in our unguarded moments, such as when we're relaxed or enjoying ourselves, or feeling love for someone or something.

I want to finish this chapter with some more comments about the power of feeling good, because it is the key to *everything*.

When we take the time to *feel good first*, before making any decisions, before taking any actions, we open to the greater part of ourselves, which is where our creativity and courage reside, and from where comes our inspiration and our impetus to act on it.

When I don't feel good, I immediately dismiss what may be good ideas — or I don't have them at all. When I feel good, good ideas pop effortlessly into my mind; and before too long, others drop in to support or expand on them.

If I harbor any *contradictory* thoughts about what I want, such as doubting my ability to create it or my worthiness to have it, I slow or even subvert my progress, and the thing I want is either very slow to materialize, or it never appears at all.

But when I feel good, I'm so sure of these good ideas that I enthusiastically head in that direction, proceeding with absolute confidence as I move steadily and inexorably toward whatever it is that I'm wanting to create.

> When we feel good, we see that we are
> already surrounded by things we love.

When we feel good, we see all the good things we already have in our lives, and that we are already surrounded by things we love, as we enjoy the prospect of receiving even more.

When I don't feel good, I may not even look around me; and if I do, I see only what I don't have. When I feel good, I'm astonished by what I already have around me, all without me even trying.

The natural world is particularly good at that cheeky little trick: no matter the season, I'm always surrounded by wonderful things I've done absolutely nothing to create, earn, or otherwise "deserve." We all are. All the time. Whether we notice it or not.

The animals we love are another great example of how we are already surrounded by lovely things.

When we feel good, we see possibilities that couldn't occur to us when we're closed off from this inspiration, when we don't feel good.

When I feel good, I see clearly where I want to go, and I fully expect to get there. I may not yet see the entire path to my destination, but the first step is obvious; and from there, the next, and the next, and the one after that... I know where I'm going, that I will inevitably arrive, and that the journey itself will be wonderful!

Our animals are a great example of how
we are already surrounded by lovely things.

When we feel good, worry just can't abide, so we proceed with confidence and enthusiasm.

Enthusiasm is infectious, so when we feel good and act from that confidence, we attract the very people who are best able to help us achieve our goals. Conversations spontaneously occur that create wonderful and helpful connections and which expand our horizons even further as others share *their* inspirations with us.

When we feel good, thoughts arise that hadn't occurred to us before, and impulses to do things that, in the moment, may seem far removed from our goal, but which, in retrospect, were the perfect next step toward our goal.

Once I surrendered to "the scenic route," these unusual or unexpected twists and turns got to be rather fun. Once I learned to trust the process and give myself over to it, things got *very* interesting! And *that* is the stuff of life!

Not only do we not need to fear or resist these unexpected occurrences, we can take them as directions, guiding us to the best path we could take to achieve our goals.

When we feel good, our goals may even change, as we imagine a much bigger life for our self than we ever could have dreamed in our closed-off state of worry, doubt, or other limitation.

> When we feel good, our goals may change
> as we imagine a much bigger life for our self.

When I'm in that open, feel-good state of mind, it's a common experience for me to have thoughts along the way that make what I started out to do even better.

Those deviations from the original course used to really bother me, as I thought they made me weak-minded, indecisive, or uncommitted. Now I look forward to these occurrences. Whether I'm writing or gardening or cooking or setting out on a hike or treating a patient, I often revise my original thought.

My first thought is just that: initial, simply a starting point. A fundamentally good idea that might be made even better, if I let it.

When we feel good, we thus start to become all that we were always meant to be. At first, we may get only brief glimpses, but the more we do it and the longer we stay there each time, the more at home we become with this greater self, this bigger life, and the less we doubt both our worthiness and its inevitability.

The more we give our small selves over to it, the faster our lives change for the better. When we become stable in this feel-good state of mind, being there most of the time, our lives are transformed into something barely imaginable and practically unrecognizable from the meager perspectives of our small selves.

> The more we give our small selves over to it,
> the faster our lives change for the better.

That is the awesome power of feeling good.

And for us animal lovers, our animals are one of the fastest and surest routes to this feel-good state. They're a path of least resistance for us because we love them.

❊❊❊

Chapter 3

Better by choice

To recap, our lives are made better by the animals we love, particularly by those with whom we share a close bond, the special ones. When we let them, they change everything because they help us get back to feeling good, and that opens the door to all manner of possibilities!

However, for many and perhaps even most of us, these moments of lightness — that wonderfully expansive feeling of love and clarity, peace and power, when we relax and smile and feel ourselves to be part of the whole universe — are only *occasional* and *fleeting*.

In our busy and at times hectic lives, with their endless demands and distractions, we too often ignore these beautiful moments. We quickly dismiss them or rush on past them as our scattered mind grasps onto something more "important" or urgent or otherwise compelling. Or we let ourselves feel them only on the weekend or on vacation. And all too often, we miss these moments altogether.

But once we realize their importance, their tremendous power and their practical value to us, we can choose to *cultivate* these moments — to *look* for them and *revel* in them, as often and for as long as we can.

We can start by simply *noticing* when we feel good, and reminding ourselves of the power and value of this state of mind (and body). We can then *savor* the feeling, letting it linger for as long as we can before our well-practiced habits of thought intrude and rob us of that lovely, lively peace we feel when we're in that wonderful state.

> We can choose to *cultivate* these moments,
> to *look* for them and *revel* in them.

As we linger, we can let ourselves *slow down* for awhile, and come to some much-needed rest and relaxation, as we contemplate what it is that we want to do next. When we have a question we need answered or a decision to make, big or small, we can deliberately use the time we spend with our animals to help us get back to feeling good. *Then* ask, *then* decide, and *then* act.

Taking the time to relax and feel good is a sure way to let inspiration flow, along with the confidence needed to act on any ideas that occur to us in that expansive state. It's the only way that great ideas can pop into my mind. I'm sure I'm not the only one who experiences these moments of expansion and inspiration when I'm in the shower, driving a familiar route, or taking a walk.

"Necessity" may be "the mother of invention," but we still need to create enough space in our mind for something new to be conceived.

The longer I can linger in that space, the bigger or clearer
the idea becomes and the more confidence I have in it, and
in myself. Before long, other ideas appear which support it,
so I'm more willing and able to act on the inspiration. I'm
also less inclined to give up too soon when the outcome
I envision doesn't immediately materialize or doesn't look
the way I thought it would or think it should.

In other words, the more often I find myself in that feel-good
state and the longer I stay there each time, the more trust
I have in the ideas that occur to me there, and the more likely
the thing is to become a reality, because I'm better able
to proceed with confidence and competence toward it.

> The longer I can linger in that space,
> the more likely the idea is to become a reality.

I dearly wish I'd known all this when Miss Lilly was alive.
I missed far too many of her subtle — and some not-so-subtle
— hints and her wonderful reminders of the supreme
importance of play and silliness, and of rest and relaxation,
of the simple joy of sitting on the front steps in the morning
sunshine as the world hurries on by — in other words,
the importance of feeling good.

Still, she persisted, and I unwittingly let her lead me into
feeling good, or at least feeling better. Many's the time Miss
Lilly got me up off the couch or away from the computer
to take a walk, go for a hike or a swim in the lake, or play
a game of tug-o'-war with one of her toys. I even enjoyed
picking up all of the "dog snow" (the white, synthetic fiber
filling of dog toys) from the yard, because she got such

enjoyment out of tearing it from her toys and removing their squeakers. I loved to watch her play and to go racing around in the yard like a mad thing, her tongue lolling out and a gigantic grin on her face. It never failed to make me smile, because her joy was infectious.

She also loved it when we did our farm chores, which were a twice-daily delight for the both of us in her senior years, and when I spent hours outside in the garden or doing yard work. She was always fully engaged with life, whereas I was perpetually distracted by my mental churn. All of these outdoor activities were a breath of fresh air for me, literally and figuratively, and they encouraged my mind to relax and wander freely or simply to idle.

Our animals understand the importance of play, silliness, relaxation, joy — of *feeling good.*

I didn't realize it at the time, but I had my best ideas when I was in that state of mind.

I didn't always act on those ideas, though; I didn't always trust them. Before long, the self-doubt would creep back in and erase both the good feeling and the inspiration.

Now I know to trust those ideas, and to act on them when and how I'm inspired, no questions asked.

That's how Miss Lilly lived her life. Some would say that, being "just a dog," she was merely acting on instinct. Perhaps. But what is instinct anyway? I'm now fairly sure that her mind, being less cluttered by troublesome thoughts than mine, was more open to inspiration, on which she acted without hesitation and with absolute trust. I could even see it happening in real time, as an idea occurred to her and she'd light up, change course, and do something even more fun. If that's "instinct," then make mine a double!

I had this absolutely *stellar* life coach, business coach, relationship coach, and personal trainer, all rolled into one, yet I didn't recognize her as such. To me, she was just an odd-looking stray dog who needed a home, and whom I came to love with all my heart.

> Miss Lilly needed me to recognize, cultivate, and *harness* the times when I felt good.

Because I loved her, I did my best to make her life as good as it could be. However, I completely failed to realize that what she most needed from me was for me to take good care of *myself* and to recognize, cultivate, and *harness* the times when I felt good.

It should go without saying that we don't always feel good. Neither do our animals. In fact, I don't think we *can* always feel good — at least, not in this lifetime. Feeling good all the time might even be a good definition of death, the eternal state of joyful being that precedes and succeeds this lifetime. So, while I'll get there eventually, I'm in no hurry!

We can enjoy *awareness* all the time, though, and that is something I practice (because for me it still takes practice). I still have ebbs and flows in my emotional state — and that's a good thing. It's how we're made.

We have very subtle and sophisticated sensory systems, including the biochemicals that the pioneering neuroscientist Candace Pert, PhD called our "molecules of emotion." This system warns us of potential harm and gives us affirmative feedback when we're on the right track.

Even warnings about imaginary harms are useful because they show us where we may be holding ourselves back. This system exists not just to keep us alive and protect us from harm, but to guide us throughout life and enable us to *thrive,* to imagine, create, recreate, and enjoy our lives — because we really are meant to *enjoy* our lives.

We don't always feel good,
but we can always enjoy *awareness.*

I now define 'awareness' as seeing it all and loving both the lightness and the darkness equally; as seeing the value and the preciousness of every experience, both "good" and "bad." What remains, then, is simply to express my preference in any given moment: for something I *do* want (the *Yes)* rather than for something I *don't* want (the *No).*

In other words, do I want to go on spending most of my time in survival mode, bracing against the next blow (real or imagined), when not doing everything I can to avoid it? Or do I want to focus on thriving, on really *living?*

"Well, duh!" as the kids say. I want to cultivate the habit of *looking* for these moments of brightness and *reveling* in them. I want to master the harnessing of their tremendous power to shape the life I want.

But first I needed to learn how to politely ignore everyone else. I needed to free myself from the perpetual bind of seeking others' approval and avoiding their disapproval — because therein lay a primary reason my default setting was to be stuck in survival mode. As time went on, it felt as though life just kept batting me back and forth like a well-fed cat playing with a mouse...

In meditation recently, I pondered what, for me, is a recurring problem: *how to get unstuck.* Because when I'm really stuck, in a perpetual state of anxiety or depression, or even just the blander versions of worry or boredom — the doldrums — it doesn't seem as though I have any choice in the matter at all. I just feel *trapped,* stuck, unable to move in any direction.

> I begin by acknowledging that I'm stuck
> and that I want to be *un*stuck.

I still have some deeply ingrained beliefs that keep tripping me up; and seemingly without warning, they grab hold of me and hang on like grim death. I wanted to know how to free myself when I'm in that state, struggling in vain to break free.

I have two basic strategies that work for me. On the surface, they appear to be opposites, but they both take me to the same place of lightness, of freedom, of *feeling good.*

Both begin with me acknowledging that I'm stuck on a restricting thought, a limiting belief, something I don't want (circumstance, feeling, whatever) — and that I want to be *un*stuck. In other words, I express my desire to be *free.*

But here, the two strategies diverge — for a bit...

Strategy 1. I came up with this approach many years ago, during the story I'll share in the next chapter, and out of sheer desperation, because nothing else had worked. I still use it occasionally, although less and less the more I use strategy 2.

When nothing else has worked, I take myself off somewhere quiet and give the stuck feeling my full attention. Whether I'm feeling anxious or depressed, or some other unpleasant stuckness, the process is the same. I sit and just feel all that I'm feeling in that moment, resisting the temptation to try to change it or make it disappear, both of which are futile.

When I let go by giving these feelings
my full attention, *they let me go.*

At the same time, I pay attention to the words or images that pop into my mind. Again, I don't try to change any of it or make it disappear — no matter how much I want it all to go away and never come back! I simply give it my full attention, for as long as it takes, which feels like a thousand years but in fact may be just a morning, and often far less.

It takes a willingness to stay there with those uncomfortable thoughts and feelings when it feels like they'll suffocate me, because my tendency is to try to squirm my way free. But just like when your fingers are stuck in a Chinese finger trap, the more I struggle to be free, the tighter I'm bound.

When I let go by giving these troublesome feelings my full attention, something remarkable happens: *they let me go.*

The stuck feeling begins to change and at last to dissolve
as I pay attention to the message it has for me about
whichever habit or belief is holding me back this time.

Strategy 2. With this second approach, I likewise begin by
acknowledging that I'm stuck and that I want to be *un*stuck.
But as it's always the same ol' stuff these days, I resist the
temptation to analyze it, debate it, or examine its origins.

It's enough to acknowledge that I want to be *free*. In fact,
by focusing on the problem, it's all I see; any solution is
obscured, unavailable to me in that moment.

> Simply by focusing my attention
> on what I *do* want, I'm a little *less stuck*.

Next, I direct my attention to the little bit of space that opens
up around that booger-y stuckness. Simply by focusing my
attention on being *un*stuck — on what I *do* want, on finding
something to say *Yes* to — I'm a little *less stuck*.

Simply by turning your head a little, you change your point
of view. That little bit of space around the stuckness was
always there; I just couldn't see it when all of my focus
was on what I *don't* like, on what I *don't* want, on a *No!*

From there, it's just a matter of focusing more of my attention
on what I *do* want and to start *savoring* some aspect of it that
really appeals or that is easiest for me to appreciate about it.
Then I suck the proverbial marrow out of it; really enjoy the
flavor of it, to stick with the marrow metaphor.

In this way, I'm directing my attention away from the thing I *don't* want, on which I'm so stuck, and toward the thing I *do* want instead.

Admittedly, it takes some practice, because the habit of focusing so intently on what I *don't* like or *don't* want is so strong. That habit is still my default setting, so I still need to keep noticing when I'm stuck and taking these deliberate steps to get *un*stuck. Letting go is effortless when I catch myself early and promptly shift my attention away from the thing I *don't* want onto something I *do* want.

It's all about *where,* on *what,* I give my attention.
Because it *is* a choice.

In effect, I'm changing the thing my mind is grabbing onto. When my mind is spasming — or so it feels, clenched with a vicelike grip — around some unpleasant thought, *no* amount of determination or urging or straining or struggling to let go can get my mind to let go. That's because my entire focus, all of my attention, is grabbing onto that thing, even though I don't like it and I *really* don't want it.

So, the key is to shift my focus onto something or some aspect of the present situation that I *do* want, onto a *Yes!*

One might call this 'the law of attention': whatever I give my attention to is what I experience foremost. That's not to say that other things aren't happening or present at the same time; they are. *Everything* — good, bad; wanted, unwanted — is present in this, and every, moment. It's all about *where,* on *what,* I give my attention. Because it *is* a choice.

So, little by little, I shift my attention away from what I *don't* want, to what I *do* want; from a *No* to a *Yes!* With practice, it becomes easier to do, and less of a big deal, as I catch my focus early enough that big shifts are seldom necessary, even with the "big ticket" items, the things that always trip me up and mess me up.

Over time, I become focused on what I *do* want more of the time. That's when great things start to happen.

Miss Lilly made me feel a little better, and from there a little better, and a little better still.

Even before I knew all this, I was inadvertently practicing it a bit, thanks to Miss Lilly. When I felt good already, she could make me feel *great* as she wheedled me into playing one of her favorite games or going for a walk together.

I could never go from feeling bad (depressed or angry or frustrated or disheartened) to feeling good in the blink of an eye. But Miss Lilly seldom failed to make me feel a little better, if only for her benefit, and from there a little better and a little better, and a little better still. Before I knew it, we were outside playing or taking a walk or doing something else she loved.

Because I loved her and I wanted her to be happy, I generally gave her my attention when she asked for it — and that did us both good. Every degree of improvement in my state of mind was good for me, and it was good for her.

***

Chapter 4

Better in return

When we feel good, our animals' lives are made better, because they too thrive on feeling good, particularly on feeling loved and cherished. In addition, when we feel good, we're a lot easier to live with. We take better care of ourselves and of everything else in our lives, especially those we love. We're more attuned to our animals' needs and we're better able to attend to those needs. So, all of this works to *their* benefit as well.

I must admit here that I had some help in writing this book: a fluffy cat, who lives in my imagination, steadfastly sitting to my right, waiting for me to return to the computer and finish the book. Whenever I'd get mired in the mental toil of it, I'd take a break, which sometimes stretched into weeks. No matter what, the fluffy cat patiently waited for me to be ready to get back to it. This cat also kept me on track whenever I got lost in the past.

One day when I was particularly bogged down, I asked this cat what she most wants me to say; what this book is really all about from our animals' perspective. Here is her reply:

"We want you to be happy. We *love* it when you're happy.
We *need* you to be happy.

"We are here to help you to be happy, to remind you that
your true state is happiness. We have our own lives, our own
experiences, our own interests, our own difficulties, our own
histories, our own lifespans; but we are here in yours for our
mutual benefit and our mutual *enjoyment.*

"Take full advantage of our presence, and it will make both
our lives much more enjoyable."

Ahh. So, that would make us *their* soul friends in return.
I was Miss Lilly's soul friend, and she was mine. That is,
after all, how friendship works.

Our animals *love* it when we're happy;
they *need* us to be happy.

As the fluffy cat pointed out, our animals have their own
lives, and that includes their own stresses and their own
needs. Even if we bred them ourselves and thus have known
them from birth, our animals arrive with their own histories,
partly genetic inheritance and partly acquired through life
experience. In addition to the particular requirements of their
species, they have their own personalities, proclivities, and
interests, their own challenges and difficulties, and their own
lifespans and experiences of birth and death.

Miss Lilly was having her own experience of life as a dog,
as this dog in particular, while I was having my own
experience of life as a human, as this human in particular.

I was experiencing things she wasn't, and *vice versa*. There were considerable similarities and a good deal of overlap, but significant differences as well.

The parts of our shared life, our little two-circle Venn diagram, that didn't overlap were just as important as the parts that did — perhaps even more so, because those were the parts that I didn't understand very well, and where most of Miss Lilly's particular challenges lay.

The parts of our shared life that didn't overlap were just as important as the parts that did.

When I adopted her, Miss Lilly had a permanent kink in her tail, the result of a fracture or dislocation that had healed imperfectly, creating a 90-degree bend about halfway along her tail. It wasn't painful to touch, having long ago healed with a strong callus, but still she didn't like anyone touching her tail. She also hated being picked up and carried; she'd go all stiff-legged and wide-eyed, and she wouldn't or couldn't relax until she'd been placed back down on the ground or into the car, as the case may be.

This next thing is a bit embarrassing to admit — although in my defense, her stripes acted as camouflage... She'd been living with me for several days before I noticed that she had a broad depression on the left side of her face, evidently the result of past trauma, perhaps something that had occurred at the same time as her tail injury. The plane of her upper and lower jaws was permanently tilted as a result. Clearly, something bad had happened to her when she was a puppy.

I managed this evidence of her traumatic past by assiduously ignoring it and proceeding as though it was all in the past; and for the most part, it was. She would start to snuffle and sneeze a bit if I'd gotten … hmm, let's say "a little behind" in my housework. (I love a clean, tidy house but I hate doing housework. So, I must admit that Miss Lilly's snuffling was too often my cue that I'd once again neglected the dusting and the vacuuming for too long.)

I stumbled upon this willful-blindness approach (to her past, not to the dust — well, that, too ☺) quite by accident, because I *so* didn't want to think about what might have happened to her. (*Why* do our minds tend to go to the darkest, most painful places?!)

> With each retelling of the painful past,
> we're ensuring that it stays alive and current.

But now I use it deliberately and proactively. Pretty much everyone I've ever met who has a "rescue" dog or cat or horse or hamster has very quickly launched into a detailed retelling of the tale of woe that is their "poor thing's" past. I used to listen politely, commiserating in all the right places about how awful some humans are...

Then one day I realized that with each retelling of the painful past, we're ensuring that it stays alive and current. It lingers like a bad smell, spoiling our enjoyment of the present and stunting or otherwise deforming the relationship by ensuring that the animal always remains a "poor thing" in the eyes of their person and everyone else they might meet.

Now, I politely cut in before the person really gets up a head of steam, and I try to focus their attention on the present in some way and on the wonderful things the animal brings into their life, of which there are invariably many.

I'm not always successful at changing the course of the conversation; for one reason or another, most people love to retell their animal's tragic story. But when I am, it does us all good, because it changes us humans for the better and it relegates the animal's past *to* the past, where it belongs.

Focus on the present and the wonderful things
your animal brings into your life.

All that said, we may still need to give due consideration to an individual's medical history, and accommodate any sensitivities and preferences/aversions that may have deep roots, and even genetic underpinnings, such as being noise sensitive or fearful toward strangers or new situations.

Miss Lilly was very noise sensitive, being highly reactive to short, sharp, loud noises such as gunshots, fireworks, thunder cracks, engine backfires, pneumatic nail guns, and even someone dropping a plank of wood onto a hard surface.

Lightning and flashing lights (*e.g.,* the ones on emergency vehicles) also made her very anxious. She could become inconsolably distressed during a violent thunderstorm, and just the sound of an approaching storm rumbling away in the distance would set her pacing and panting. I came to dread the Fourth of July and New Year's Eve because she became so upset during the fireworks.

I love a good storm, and fireworks — heck, my birthday is July 4th ! — so it was always a point of frustration and disappointment to me, a personal and professional failing, that I was of no comfort whatsoever to Miss Lilly during these events she found so distressing.

I just never found a way in to let her know she was safe and that all really was well. I did my best to remain calm and relaxed myself, to model unconcern and even enjoyment. But being a highly sensitive person myself, her anxiety would made me tense without realizing it, and I'd become frustrated and even exasperated that I couldn't calm her. For all my good intentions, I wasn't helping matters and sometimes I probably made things worse for her.

> For all my good intentions, I wasn't helping and sometimes I made things worse for her.

Later in her life, when she was 11 or 12 years old, I stumbled upon a solution which worked surprisingly well for us: a home-made alternative to the ThunderShirt®, consisting of two stable bandages (leg wraps for horses) which wrapped her body snugly and held her tight. Once her wrap was on, she'd settle down and even sleep through the storm or the fireworks. It was amazing!

So, a huge *thank you!* to whoever first had the idea to calm the sympathetic nervous system in this way; it was inspired! And *thank you!* to those who were inspired by this idea to develop calmwear for kids and the ThunderShirt® for dogs. These marvelous innovations by others made all the difference to us.

Speaking of sensitivity, Miss Lilly came with several dietary sensitivities, which I discuss in my book *Feeding Miss Lilly*. She was also vulnerable to fleas and very sensitive to flea bites (hypersensitivity to flea saliva). When I first met her, she was covered in fleas and ticks, so external parasites were evidently a weak spot in her defenses. Another thing I noticed was how she would swell spectacularly whenever she had what should have been just a local infection.

So, for all her bully appearance and confident front, she was a very sensitive dog with several vulnerabilities. The same could be said of me, so I understood and just accepted her sensitivities and vulnerabilities.

"When the student is ready, the teacher appears." My teacher appeared in the guise of a stray dog.

Over time, they became less and less of an issue. In part, that was because I was so focused on getting and keeping her in great health, so her system as a whole became more robust and resilient. But I think it was also because I didn't make a big deal of her sensitivities. I didn't pathologize her, the things about her that were quintessentially *her*. They were just things we were to learn about along the way.

Miss Lilly turned out to be a splendid teacher. I learned so much from her that this is the fourth book I've written which is inspired by her life. There's an oft-repeated saying in Zen Buddhism: "When the student is ready, the teacher will appear." I must have been ready, because my teacher appeared — cleverly in the guise of a stray dog.

Aggression toward other dogs was another (and perhaps related) issue, most of all because it was inconsistent. I was never able to predict which dogs Miss Lilly would like and accept and which she would try to dominate and even attack. She was often, but not always, the instigator; and regardless of who started it, she always "gave as good as she got." Miss Lilly was involved in a few memorable dog fights that still upset me to think about all these years later.

When we were out, I seldom let her off-leash unless I was sure there were no strange dogs around. I became so reactive to dogs we didn't know that I'm sure I made things worse and increased the potential for conflict — between the two dogs and between me and the other dog's person.

> She held up a mirror to my sensitivity
> and reactivity to other people.

Thinking back, she was holding up a mirror to my sensitivity and reactivity to other people. If only I'd relaxed and enjoyed meeting these other dogs and their people, as Miss Lilly so often did.

For all that drama (real and imagined), Miss Lilly formed deep and lasting friendships with other dogs. She had a particular fondness for large males. She was spayed, but I still thought of those dogs as her boyfriends; they were boys and they were genuinely her friends. She loved them dearly and never had any trouble with them, nor they with her.

Her very favorite was Nicholas, a large German Shepherd Dog who belonged to one of our dear friends, Walter. Being of a similar age when they first met, she and Nicholas became instant friends and playmates, entertaining us all with their antics. Over the years, she repeated this pattern with a few other dogs, finding instant camaraderie and sustaining long and carefree friendships with them.

Miss Lilly lived quite happily with six other dogs at our home in the Seattle area. We lived on the corner lot of a group of four rental houses that had once belonged to the same family, so all of our yards were interconnected. Being renters, people came and went over the years. The final grouping of people and dogs was a delight. As all of our dogs got along well, we opened up the interior gates and created our own private dog park. Our dogs loved it, and so did we humans.

Was she showing me the high cost of letting others "get to me"?

I still miss having a kitchen full of dogs. I even miss the enterprisingly naughty Bella, an exceedingly smart young Basset Hound, deliberately messing with my stuff — particularly the things I told her not to touch, such as when she strategically unraveled a ball of my knitting yarn all through the house while I'd nipped out to run an errand.

Miss Lilly also got along well with the livestock guardian dogs (all Great Pyrenees) who protected the goats on the farm in North Carolina where we lived for the last 4–5 years of her life. So, she was a very social dog, both with people and with other dogs; it's just that some dogs rubbed her the wrong way, and her response was very canine. Or was it that she was showing me the high cost of letting others "get to me"?

As for our friend Walter, he and Miss Lilly showed me early on just how smart and discerning she was. I have zero tolerance for animals biting me, even in play, so my rule with all animals is that they must never, ever place their teeth on my skin unless it's to drag my unconscious body out of the path of oncoming traffic!

Walter, on the other hand, loved to play rough with his dogs. Being a former cop and US Coast Guardsman, and more recently a retired sea captain, he came across as a crusty old barnacle, but he was one of the kindest and most generous people I've ever known, and he loved animals.

Miss Lilly knew it was all a game, and that Walter had invited her to play it with him.

While we were visiting Walter and his wife Kim one weekend, I noticed how much Miss Lilly enjoyed it when Walter would invite her to grab his arm, like attack dogs are trained to do, and pretend to maul him. At first, I was aghast! But I quickly realized that Miss Lilly knew it was all a game, and that Walter had invited her to play it with him. He'd set the parameters, and she was happy to play within them. She was utterly delighted by the whole thing, and with Walter calling her Tiger instead of Lilly.

And what an interesting metaphor… The way I see things now, we are all playing an elaborate game here in this lifetime, and we choose to play within the parameters set out for us (for our species, by our family, our culture, and our time). Yet again, Miss Lilly is showing me something important, something I had long forgotten.

Now back to our story. I told her that I wouldn't *ever* want to play that attack game, but I was happy for her to play it with Walter if they both wanted. She never once tried to play it with me; it was just a game she played with Walter, and no-one else. I took the view that she could create her own rules with each of the people in our life, and I wouldn't interfere. From then on, her relationships with each of our friends and neighbors were unique, as gentle or boisterous as the person preferred.

Over time, the list of people who offered to take her off my hands if anything ever happened to me — to which I would think, "What do you mean, 'if anything ever happens to me'? Just what are you planning?!" — or if I had to return to Australia grew to a disconcerting length. They volunteered this information; it wasn't in response to any anxiety I'd voiced. In short, they wanted my dog!

> Her relationships with each of our friends
> and neighbors were unique.

Miss Lilly could also tell time and read minds — or perhaps her ability to tell time was really about her ability to read my mind.

Here's an example: I was working at my computer late one afternoon when Miss Lilly wandered into my office and very politely suggested that it was time to stop for the day and take our walk. She was always very polite about these interruptions, but also very clear. I was in the middle of something "important" — I can't remember what it was, that's how important it actually was — so I said to her,

"Give me 30 minutes to finish this, and then we'll go."

She sighed, turned, walked into the living room, and lay down. Thirty minutes later, to the minute, she was back. I was so astonished that I nearly fell off my chair! I thought her remarkable timeliness deserved rewarding, so I shut down my computer and went for a walk with her.

What has stayed with me is not the "important" thing I was working on, but the surprise and delight I felt at Miss Lilly's uncanny presence of mind, and her presence in general.

At the end of this book I've included two more short stories about Miss Lilly which I've already published as blog posts. But one more story is worth telling.

> What stayed with me was Miss Lilly's uncanny presence of mind, and her presence in general.

As I mentioned, in her final years we lived on a small farm in North Carolina. During several springs, I raised a handful of day-old chicks because I really like keeping hens for their fresh eggs. Being an avid hunter, Miss Lilly was fascinated by them. Concerned that she might harm them, I told her that they weren't for eating; they were going to grow up and make us eggs, so we must take good care of them. But I needn't have worried; she never attempted to harm them. In fact, she seemed to understand the mission very well...

Needing to be kept warm, the chicks lived in the laundry, under a heat lamp, until they were fully feathered and the weather was warm enough for them to go live outside.

One year we had a particularly flighty batch of chicks.
I was working at my desk one morning when Miss Lilly
came rushing in to my office with an excited and alarmed
"Timmy's in the well!" sort of expression on her face. She
seldom barked or made any other sounds, but she had a
very expressive face. She was quite an old dog by this point,
so I hadn't seen her do anything like that in some time.

Just like Lassie — or Skippy, the Bush Kangaroo, if you were
a little Aussie kid in the late '60s — her body language urged
me to follow her. She led me to the laundry room, where
I discovered that one of those wild little chicks had figured
out how to fly and had escaped from their enclosure.

> It felt very much as though we were involved
> in the same enterprise as partners.

I thanked Miss Lilly profusely for letting me know (I was
still astonished by what she could understand about human
concerns) and I asked her to tell me if any of them do
something like that again — which she duly did, although
with less alarm and with more of a mildly exasperated
"They're at it again" sort of expression as, one by one,
the chicks realized that they too could fly.

It felt very much as though we were involved in the same
enterprise (raising chicks) as partners, and we were equally
invested in making sure our chicks survived and went on
to make us eggs.

Until the chicks were older and the weather warmed up,
I'd ferry them outside for a pick on the grass each day.

Chicks are intrepid little things, given how tasty they are to all manner of creatures (I'm told they taste like chicken), so Miss Lilly was a huge help in keeping them safe while they were outside, ranging around as chickens do. She never once tried to harm them, and I'm sure she would have vigorously defended them if it ever came to that — mostly, I think, because *I* cared about them.

I'd forgotten that when she was a much younger dog she'd shown a similar regard for an animal who would ordinarily have been her prey.

> She'd shown a similar regard for an animal who would ordinarily have been her prey.

When we moved to Seattle, we spent the first couple of weeks with Kathy, an old friend from vet school, who had moved there a few years earlier with her partner and their young child. Miss Lilly loved it there, as Kathy's daughter had a pet rat, Henry. His cage was better than Dog TV, it was like canine SmellaVision!

Curiously, though, Miss Lilly didn't ever try to eat him, even though she was a very dedicated and accomplished hunter. She was transfixed when the little girl would get Henry out of his cage to play with him. She would sniff him all over with an expression of wonder and delight, rather than of a predator's excitement at zeroing in on its prey.

Equally interesting to me, Henry never seemed to be afraid of Miss Lilly. I told her a few times when we first arrived that she must not eat him, as he was the little girl's friend.

Apparently, that made sense to her because she never bothered him, when rats in general didn't stand a chance with her. She caught and killed many a wild rat in her time.

So, Miss Lilly was a complex creature with hidden depths. I've found that to be true of pretty much all animals I've met, including Baabara, the sheep who lives next door and is way too smart for me. Baabara has learned way more about me and my habits than I have about hers!

> Our life together was more interesting
> and fun than one might suppose.

It made our life together vastly more interesting and fun than one might suppose when a dog is reduced to its general species and breed characteristics. Miss Lilly came with her own history that was likewise hidden from me (and probably just as well...). She had her own decided likes and dislikes, preferences and aversions. And she had her own health challenges and her own lifespan, which was considerably shorter than my own (hence all the fuss at the beginning).

Taking care of her was easy, given my background. But taking care of her *well* or as well as I could or should have, is where I fell down. That's because I hadn't yet learned the tremendous importance of feeling good, of catching it, cultivating it, and harnessing it for our mutual benefit.

In the revised edition of *Feeding Miss Lilly,* I wrote about a lump on her flank which I'm fairly certain was a mast cell tumor. I never did get around to doing a biopsy, but its appearance and behavior were consistent with those of a mast cell tumor, which is the most common type of skin tumor in dogs.

The lump first appeared when she was 4 or 5 years old, a few months after we'd made our first cross-country move, from Cary, North Carolina to Seattle, Washington. It disappeared spontaneously a year or so later, eating itself from the inside out. But eventually it returned, and it remained until her death at somewhere between 16 and 17 years of age.

> Miss Lilly's lump was a barometer for our (which is to say *my)* sense of well-being.

Its behavior all the while was a barometer for our (which is to say *my)* sense of well-being, and specifically our/my sense of safety and security, because those dozen years were a very bumpy ride, during which I experienced repeated bouts of severe depression and thoughts of suicide.

I want to pause for a minute and let you know what's coming up and how I've decided to approach it. I'm going to talk with unvarnished honesty about my experience with cyclic depression and suicidal thoughts, but I want to approach it with the curiosity and wonder of an explorer —a spelunker, to be specific.

Not only is discussing depression a bit like exploring an underground cave system, but 'spelunking' is a fun word and it evokes the sense of adventure and the eventual return to the surface, to the sunlight and fresh air, that I want for this little armchair adventure of ours.

So, if you'll trust me to guide you through the darkness, point out the features and the pitfalls, and bring you safely back into the light when we're done, let's continue.

Looking back, were I to have charted the fluctuations in my emotional state on the same axis as those of Miss Lilly's lump, the two wavy lines would have been pretty closely matched. Whenever we were (which is to say *I* was) particularly and protractedly stressed, whether I was predominantly anxious or depressed, her lump and the surrounding skin became reddened and swollen (signs of mast cell activation). It all settled back down again as things settled down in our lives.

> The fluctuations in my emotional state
> matched the changes in her lump.

Mast cells are interesting things. In medicine, we're used to thinking of them as being involved in the expression of allergy; and for most of us, that's about the extent of our knowledge and interest. However, mast cells are up to far more than that.

Most of them spend their adult lives at our boundaries, particularly the boundaries between our tissues and the outside world (*e.g.*, in the skin and in the walls of the digestive and respiratory tracts). So, first and foremost they are monitors and sentinels, standing guard and warning against things that might harm us.

Mast cells also play protective roles against parasites and microbes, and they actively participate in wound healing.

Even more interesting are their roles in immune tolerance, which is the discerning capability of the immune system to distinguish between friend and foe, and in the fascinating two-way communication between the goings-on in the gut and the brain (the gut–brain axis).

Unlike most other immune cells, mast cells are normally found in the brain, doing for the brain what they do for the rest of us. There is also a well-established link between the skin, the gut, and the brain. And why not? Everything is connected to everything else in the body, and it all works — and breaks down — as an integrated whole.

> Miss Lilly's sophisticated sensory system was sending me updates about how safe she felt.

So, in the form of a small, pink, hairless lump on the side of her belly, Miss Lilly's highly sophisticated sensory system was sending me updates about how safe (or not) she felt at any given time. And I missed them. Oh, I noticed them, of course; I even worried about them at times. But I didn't appreciate their significance or their value to us.

How interesting that the medical research field pioneered by Dr Candace Pert, author of *Molecules of Emotion* and *Everything You Need to Know to Feel Go(o)d*, is called psycho-neuro-immunology. I read both books while all this was going on, and still I missed Miss Lilly's messages to me, manifested in her skin by her own molecules of emotion.

I occasionally attempted to make the lump or the swelling in the surrounding tissue disappear, because I didn't like it being there; but I was missing the whole point of its existence and its behavior. Miss Lilly would have been better served by me attending to my own life, to the things that stressed *me*, because *I* became the thing that stressed *her* the most.

The move to Seattle in the spring of 2005 was inspired, what I thought of as "meant to be," and I was very excited at the prospect of moving out there and starting my own holistic veterinary practice in such metaphorically fertile soil. I jokingly blamed the undersea earthquake which spawned that devastating tsunami in the Indian Ocean on Boxing Day (December 26) 2004 for joggling something loose in the ethers, because I woke up a few days later, on New Year's Day 2005, with the thought, "Oh, I gotta to move to Seattle!"

I became the thing that stressed her the most.

That was a completely new thought to me. I'd never been there, and at the time I didn't even know anyone who lived there, yet it was as plain as day that I should move out there, and to this day I don't question the wisdom of it. For all the trouble that ensued, it kicked off a truly wonderful time in my life, and I still miss living there.

As I waited for spring to arrive so the interstate highways in the Midwest and the northwestern states would be clear of snow (a route and strategy a professional trucker advised), I set about packing up my old life. That gave me a few months to think about this big move — to somewhere I'd never been, to do something I'd never done (start my own practice) — so of course I did rethink it, many times. What was I doing, making such a move on faith alone?!

65

Whenever I doubted the wisdom of my decision, I'd think to myself, "Well, you can always stay put." But every time, that thought filled me with such a leaden feeling that I knew I needed to go. It was the right thing for me to do, and the right time for me to do it. That heavy feeling left me in no doubt as to which way I should go.

Thus began the most difficult and dangerous period of my life, as I'll explain. (Remember that we'll be coming up for air once I'm done. Note, too, that I did survive it all. ☺)

I started out feeling very excited and only a little nervous about the move, and I had absolute faith in what I was embarking on, knowing with complete certainty that I would succeed. "How hard can it be?" I thought, "its meant to *be!*"

I became frustrated and discouraged when
what I wanted was slow to materialize.

But the reality turned out to be very different. I'm naturally (or is that just habitually?) an impatient person. I also have a strong perfectionist streak, so of course I'm perennially plagued by an excess of self-judgement, self-criticism, and self-doubt. That proved to be a very destructive combination.

Within a week of our arrival, I began to get frustrated and at times discouraged because what I'd wanted and was so looking forward to having was slow to materialize, no matter how hard I tried, no matter how much I pushed and pulled.

(Can you see the problem already?)

It took me awhile to find us a suitable place to live, and we ended up staying in four different places in the space of about three months. I'm a real homebody, so all that moving was unsettling for me, and evidently for Miss Lilly as well, because her lump first appeared shortly after our fourth relocation.

It was also disheartening, because I'd had a clear picture in my mind of the house we'd be living in — what I wanted — ever since I'd had the idea to move to Seattle. And, of course, this move was inspired and meant to be, so surely the way would be clear and doors would open for me, when and how I wanted.

> The *feel* of that wonderful old house
> was *exactly* what I'd wanted.

The house I eventually found for us had several of the features I'd been envisioning, and it suited us well overall, but it looked nothing like the place I'd imagined and it was way more expensive than I'd wanted. I grew to love it, though, and it worked out very well for us — so much so that I distressed Miss Lilly when I burst into great, sobbing tears as we were driving away from it in a U-Haul truck five years later, in the first of several moves over the next two awful years… But I'm jumping ahead.

It wasn't until many years later that I realized the *feel* of that wonderful old house was *exactly* what I'd been wanting, not its appearance, its location, or any other physical features that had initially disappointed me.

The same thing has happened since with other places where I've lived. Each house came to feel *exactly* like what I wanted, even though it didn't start out that way.

I finally realized that it was *me and Miss Lilly* who made our house into the home I came to love. But that realization was still a long way off at the time.

It also took much longer than I'd expected for my veterinary practice to grow. It was one frustration, one disappointment, after another — at least, that's the way I saw it at the time.

> It was *me and Miss Lilly* who made our house
> into the home I came to love.

I'd been a veterinarian for over twenty years at that point. I had two postgraduate degrees and two residencies at veterinary teaching hospitals under my belt, and I'd been focused on holistic medicine for six years, so I was ready to have my own practice. I'd also worked as a freelance medical writer and editor for over ten years, so while I'm no business expert, I was no stranger to running my own business.

I just couldn't understand my lack of success, given that the plan was inspired, meant to be, and I was following it faithfully — or so I thought.

I see now that what I thought and how I felt were determined by what was happening around me, especially by the people around me, and by my self-judgement — by what I *thought* people were thinking about me, when in reality they most likely weren't giving me much thought at all.

Apparently, what others thought, or what I *thought* they thought, was more important than what *I* thought. What I was thinking and how I was feeling in any given moment always seemed to be subject to what was happening around me, so it felt as though my thoughts and feelings were largely out of my control, because the things around me were largely out of my control.

I didn't yet know that I could catch my thoughts and the feelings associated with them early, when I was just starting on the downward slide, and redirect my focus from what I don't want or what I fear might happen to what I *do* want and what I look forward to happening.

> I didn't yet know how to redirect
> my focus to what I *do* want.

I hadn't yet learned how to quietly ignore the opinions and habits — which is to say, the *beliefs* — of others and go my own way, no matter what others were saying or doing.

I hadn't yet figured out how to create a bubble of calm confidence around myself that resists all thoughts to the contrary, and thus becomes self-sustaining and self-fulfilling.

If I'd known all that, if I'd known how to take care of what was going on *inside* me, I'd have been better able to remain focused on my goals and to make better decisions. Instead, I unwittingly let people and circumstances keep me ping-ponging between optimism and pessimism, faith and frustration, confidence and doubt, and as time went on, hope and despair.

When things were going well, I felt great! I was inspired,
optimistic, enthusiastic, and energetic. Not surprisingly,
I was very productive during these times.

In addition to my veterinary practice, I created a collection
of herbal blends and natural supplements for horses and
other animals, and I later published the recipes as a book.
I also created a collection of water-based herbal essences that
were inspired by herbal medicine, homeopathy, and music.
And I wrote many articles for animal health and equestrian
magazines.

> When things were going well, I felt great
> and Miss Lilly thrived.

Throughout, I continued medical writing and editing,
contributing to numerous clinical research papers, textbooks,
and conference proceedings. And I wrote and published two
more books: one on caring for our animals and ourselves
(*Nothing More is Needed*) and a few years later the first edition
of *Feeding Miss Lilly*.

That's the tremendous power of feeling good. And during
those times, Miss Lilly thrived.

But when things did *not* go the way I wanted, the way
I thought they should, I felt the opposite. At first, feelings
of impatience and frustration predominated, with short
but predictable dips into discouragement as I began to doubt
myself. As time went on, the feeling that began to dominate
was disappointment, which gave way by degree to sadness,
despondency, and finally a sense of hopelessness.

My bouts of depression became so severe that I could barely function when they took over. I felt like I was suffocating in a dense, grey fog or I was trapped down a deep, dark well, because there seemed to be no way out.

I would always see to Miss Lilly's physical needs (food, water, toilet, walks), however, so she kept me going during those times. But at what cost to her?

As I mentioned in the prologue, I'd made a promise when I adopted her that I would take good care of her for the rest of her life, and I'm glad to say that I never once let her down, at least in regard to her *physical* needs. In fact, it was good to have a reason to get out of bed those mornings, and tending to her needs made me feel useful for those few minutes.

> Depression is wanting something I don't have and don't believe I *can* have or *will* get.

But what did it cost her to take good care of me during those times? Her lump indicated that, during my dark periods, she was very stressed, too.

I've thought a lot about depression over the years, wanting to understand its underpinnings. The way I now think of depression is this: it's the inevitable result of wanting something I don't have and don't believe I *can* have or *will* get, despite my best efforts.

The intensity of the wanting is reflected in the depth of the feeling associated with its lack. If it's something I think might simply be nice to have, then I may just feel a bit flat at the

71

thought of not being able to have it or get it. But if it's something I really want or think I really need — or that is meant to *be* — then not having it becomes a major, and even all-consuming, dilemma. And for me, it triggered an existential crisis.

A key element is the contradictory thoughts I have about the thing I really want: I want it or I think I need it, but I don't think I can have it or will get it.

How can anyone *not* be depressed by that insoluble problem? I can't stop *wanting* it, yet I can see no way of *getting* it, and I may not even think I *deserve* it, otherwise I would already have it or be in the process of getting it.

A key element is the contradictory thoughts
I have about the thing I really want.

The experience of severe depression was entirely new to me, so I had no tools for managing it nor the thoughts of suicide which became such an attractive solution.

Intelligent person that I am and a holistic practitioner with an interest in spiritual things, I thought I should be able to get past it myself, so I didn't seek professional help, nor did I take any antidepressants (unless one counts chocolate… and one should *always* count chocolate! ☺).

The couple of veterinary colleagues to whom I bared my soul during those times (both holistic practitioners as well) were no help, and their slightly alarmed expression and evident unease with my distress only made me feel worse.

What the heck was wrong with me?! Thank goodness for
Miss Lilly! I would not leave her, so I battled on.

Another key factor for me was my impatience, how long the
thing I wanted was taking to materialize. I would repeatedly
think, with great aggravation, "Where *is* it; why isn't it *here*
yet?!", this thing, this new life, that had been so inspired,
so meant to be.

Now I know that the material appearance of the thing I want
may take some time, because it is the *completion* of the process
of creating something from an idea, the *end result*. Trusting
in the process and reveling in the *idea* of the thing and in
its gradual unfolding or emergence is just as important as
— in fact, it's *elemental* to — getting to enjoy the thing itself.

> Reveling in the *idea* and its gradual unfolding
> is *elemental* to getting to enjoy the thing itself.

Now I know that it's a myth that success takes hard work
and a long time. Hard work, great effort, unpleasant or
uncomfortable toil is *not* required when inspiration fuels
the action. A long time is *not* required when one redefines
success as the steady and joyful unfolding of the thing I want.

I didn't know that at the time. The process brought me no joy
because I kept looking past each little step, each new client,
each published article, each recovered patient — past the
present moment and the present indications that it is indeed
on the way. I looked only to the end result and fretted that
it wasn't fully realized yet. In my mind, all I saw was that
money, and therefore time, was running out.

Time — at least, my *perception* of it — began to tyrannize me. I was still relying on a small-business loan and credit cards to keep me afloat, my savings having been depleted in the move, buying the equipment and supplies I needed to open my practice, and all the other expenses involved in starting and supporting a new business until it's well on its feet.

One could say that I was under-capitalized, and that's why I failed. I would say now that I was not sufficiently practiced at proceeding on faith, on trusting the process and reveling in the steady unfolding of my venture.

> I spent too little time in the feel-good state
> from which all good things flow.

As I slipped further and further into debt, I found it harder and harder to remain positive. The practice slowly grew through 2006–2007, but unbeknown to me the bottom was about to fall out of the global economy like a wet cardboard box. Already the US economy was slowing.

"The economy" was a very convenient excuse for my failure, so it was most aggravating to see others succeeding and even thriving under the same conditions I found so depressing. It wasn't just the shrewd or unscrupulous "money guys" who were thriving; it was all sorts of people, in all walks of life. What was that about?! How could others be thriving while I was going under?

In short, I spent too little time in the feel-good state from which all good things flow: inspiration, practical ideas, confidence, and constancy.

74

Not surprisingly, my serial frustration, discouragement, and despondency became self-fulfilling because we don't make good decisions in those states. We end up making decisions that, inadvertently, keep things the same or make things worse.

Currently, I'm living in a beautiful rural area in the hills outside of Melbourne. I'm about a mile and a half from our little town. I could walk to the grocery store if I needed, although it's uphill most of the way, an invigorating walk that really gets the heart pumping.

The view is lovely all the way, and spectacular in places. Were I to walk to the store, I could stop at any point along the way and take a short break while enjoying the scenery, before continuing on to my destination, which really isn't all that far away and is well within my reach.

> If only I'd been able to see that the view is lovely all the way, and spectacular in places.

What I would be a fool to do is fret the whole way, grumbling that I'm not there yet, and wondering with exasperation how much further it is and when I will get there.

Or worse: give up halfway and sit there complaining; or turn back toward home, deeply disappointed that I never made it to my destination. Worse still: keep on heading down the hill, past my house, and even further from my destination.

Well, I ended up doing all of those counterproductive things. Over the next few years, my grand plan slowly fizzled and eventually died, and I ended up far worse off, in every way, than before I'd set out.

Although I still cycled between feeling good and feeling bad, depending on what was happening around me, I began the gradual and seemingly inexorable descent through disappointment, discouragement, and despondency, to despair. How could something so inspired fail to become fully realized?

How could it *possibly* become a reality
when most of my thoughts were to the contrary?

Well, how could it *possibly* become a reality when most of my thoughts were to the contrary?

I was so focused on what I *didn't* want, what I didn't yet *have*, or what I *worried* might happen — running out of money, making a mistake with a patient, annoying an influential client… the list is endless when a creative mind is controlled by fear — that I was spending too little time focused on what I *did* want and enjoying what I already *have*, including Miss Lilly. I must have been awful to live with during those times!

By late 2007, when the global economy was getting ready to tip into full-scale crisis, I was repeatedly plagued by bouts of deep depression and thoughts of suicide. As the global financial crisis worsened through 2008 and 2009, so did my mental-emotional health.

What had been inspired and meant to be became a source of deep disappointment, grievance ("Why is this *happening* to me? What have I done to *deserve* this?!"), and frequent dips into the bottomless pit of despair. How it didn't kill me still amazes me, and I credit Miss Lilly for keeping me going through those dark times.

Try as I might, I couldn't counteract the corrosive effects of group-think, particularly the mass fear and pessimism which characterized the global financial crisis for several years after the headlines had moved on to something else. Those negative thoughts have a way of fulfilling themselves because of the fearful, pessimistic decisions we make in that state of mind (and body). It took me over a decade to recover from the unforeseen loss of income and credit — and faith.

> Negative thoughts have a way
> of fulfilling themselves.

I gave up all pretense and all hope in September 2010 when I could no longer pay my rent. Between October 2010 and November 2012, we moved eight times, refugees of the Great Recession, which was my own personal Great Depression.

Those moves included a short relocation to southern Oregon which didn't "take" (I fled back up to Seattle three months later); a six-month period of homelessness we survived only thanks to the kindness of friends; a bleak few months in a very depressing basement apartment with awful neighbors overhead; a second cross-country relocation from the Seattle area to central North Carolina, my ears drooping and my tail between my legs; and lastly a shorter move to Miss Lilly's final address, where we lived until her death several years later, and where she is buried.

I don't like moving, but I do like nesting and setting up home, so as things would settle down after each move, so too did Miss Lilly's lump and the surrounding skin.

Every time we moved, I felt I was moving toward something I wanted as much as I was leaving behind something I didn't want, but of course Jon Kabat-Zinn is quite right: *Wherever you go, there you are* (the title of his book on mindfulness meditation in everyday life). No matter where we moved, I took my habits of thought — which is to say, my long-familiar impatience, anxieties, doubts, and fears — with me, so nothing really changed.

> No matter where we moved, I took my habits of thought with me, so nothing really changed.

It's not surprising to me now that my inconsistency resulted in the slow and inconsistent development of my practice. Particularly the things I perceived as failures, and even just the *fear* of failure, inevitably hurtled me into thoughts and feelings of failure, which of course became self-fulfilling. One cannot make good decisions that result in success when fearing or anticipating failure.

This inconsistency was also reflected in the inconsistent behavior of Miss Lilly's lump, and perhaps in her inconsistent behavior toward other dogs. There are probably other fluctuations in her physical and psychological health and well-being that I missed entirely.

Looking back, of course Miss Lilly's health and well-being were directly affected by mine. We were living in each other's space most of the time, and she was dependent on me for food, water, shelter, exercise, and company. I didn't take her with me on vet calls, but as I was operating my practice out of my home (it was a mobile practice, but my office was in my spare bedroom), and I was busy with my various other home-based activities, we spent a lot of time together.

So, the fact that Miss Lilly was able to keep her lump in check until she was a very old dog is fascinating to me. Assuming that it was a low-grade mast cell tumor, and as it was a solitary lump when it first appeared, she could have been expected to live a normal lifespan after complete surgical excision, which involves removal of the tumor and some surrounding skin to minimize the risk of recurrence.

Miss Lilly's health and well-being were directly affected by mine.

But I did not remove it, so it should have continued to grow and even spread to other sites. It did eventually spread to the lymph nodes in her groin, but she lived for another five years after that. She lived a normal lifespan without treatment.

She might have lived even longer if I'd removed it as soon as it appeared, or at any time before it spread. But she might instead have made new ones or manifested her life stresses in other ways that may not have been as easy for her to keep in check or for me to recognize.

I was reminded recently that it's fairly common for new mast cell tumors of a higher grade (more likely to be malignant) to appear after surgical excision, so removing that solitary lump may not have done her any favors. I'll never know for sure, and I even wonder how much it really matters in the grand scheme of things...

From a purely material/physical perspective, she was an ordinary dog, living an ordinary dog's life, which lasted longer than some, not as long as others, and nowhere near as long as I'd have liked. She arrived with her own history, her own personality, and her own perspective on life. I would now add that she also had her own *purpose.*

Clearly, as our origin story in the prologue showed, we were meant to find each other and to share our lives for a while. Unbeknown to me at the time, I was meant to scoop her up after her rough start and take good care of her for the rest of her life, as she enjoyed life as a much-loved dog.

We were each other's much-needed soul friend.

And evidently, Miss Lilly was meant to accompany me and metaphorically keep me from sinking as I navigated my way blindly through the turbulent seas of modern human life.

We were each other's much-needed soul friend, and we shared many moments we both thoroughly enjoyed, although from different perspectives and thus for different reasons.

One example was the moment when I realized what dogs like Miss Lilly find beautiful. We were living in the Seattle area at the time. On one bright, spring morning we both sat on the front porch, at the top of the steps, enjoying the sunshine. Our front yard was bordered by a six-foot tall privacy fence, and a pair of overgrown cypress trees sheltered the front gate. Along the foundation of the house was a garden bed that was filled with bluebells, nodding their beautiful mauve heads in the soft breeze.

It was mid-morning on a week day, so the street was very quiet. Miss Lilly was sitting on her haunches, looking out calmly yet attentively onto the same scene. She sniffed the air and then gave a big, contented sigh.

I got the distinct impression that, in that moment, she was experiencing beauty as order, of everything (including me) in its place and all (including me) as it should be.

Dog is in her heaven and all is right in her world.

Well, who am I to argue with that?!

Better together.

Although we took a long, rambling journey to get here, I now know this: we can *transform* our shared lives by making a decision to enjoy *more* of the lovely, lively peace we now only *sometimes* experience with our animals.

The more we do it, the easier it is to find and the longer it lasts. Over time, we gradually change our habitual setpoint to a more positive frame of mind, and all of the good things that flow from it benefit both us and the animals we love.

✳✳✳✳✳

Epilogue

As I was burying Miss Lilly's body the morning after her death, a thought popped unbidden into my quiet mind:

"We were both well loved."

It was a sweet and surprisingly matter-of-fact thought for such a somber moment.

Perhaps it's because, being a veterinarian, I'm on friendly terms with death and there was nothing alarming to me about her vacant body. I'd also been anticipating Miss Lilly's death ever since I adopted her fifteen years earlier, so by then I was well practiced at the thought of her leaving.

It still made me sad, but as I said to those who commiserated with me, I thought of her death (and still do) as "sad but good." Sad, in that I would miss her terribly; good, in that I was very glad she got to live the entire arc of her life and to leave it on her own terms. I'd been standing by, ready to euthanize her when the time came, but it never did. She died in her own time, in her own way, on her own bed, which was right next to mine, after a day I knew would be her last.

I still feel very, very blessed to have had that lovely dog, my furry soul friend, in my life for a time. I still miss her, but she left only when I was ready to go it alone. The quote I mentioned earlier about the student and the teacher is sometimes given this conclusion:

> "When the student is *truly* ready...
> the teacher will *dis*appear."

A few months ago, I was taking a walk in a local park that is frequented by dog owners. I needed to clear my head, as I was — yet again — bogged down in the past. Even before I was fully out of the car, two little old Chihuahuas toddled over. As I squatted down to say hello, one gave me a gigantic grin and a big kiss on the cheek.

"Sorry about that," his person said. "He has no sense of personal space!"

I laughed. "I don't either when it comes to animals." Truth is, I just can't keep my hands off 'em! I went on, "I'm dogless at the moment, so this is a real treat!"

"Oh, I know it well," she replied. "I was dogless for about nine years before these little ones came along."

"Yeah," I said, "I'm not worried. My next dog will show up, right on time."

She nodded and gave me a knowing smile.

*****

A couple more stories

Here are two more stories about Miss Lilly and another on applying these principles to all animals. Each is already published as a blog post, but they're worth sharing again here. Enjoy! ☺

Miss Lilly plays fetch

Years ago, when Miss Lilly was young, I was playing around with the concept of using mental imagery to communicate thoughts to animals nonverbally and nonphysically. (Do you see me trying to wriggle out of using the word 'telepathy'? ☺) I don't recall exactly what I was reading at the time, but it was around about when I read *The Field* by Lynne McTaggart.

As well-loved dogs tend to do, Miss Lilly had a toy basket that was full of all sorts of dog toys. (Yes, I was one of *those* dog owners! ☺) One was a rubber ball, a little larger than a tennis ball, that had the pentagonal soccer-ball pattern on its surface, only it was orange-and-white instead of black-and-white. To her, there was nothing particularly remarkable about it; the ball had a good 'mouth feel' (*i.e.*, it fit well in her mouth and it was fun to chew), but it wasn't her favorite toy, by any means. She'd only play with it if I got it out and threw it for her.

She was no good at playing fetch; she just didn't see the point! She loved to chase things — live things, in particular. But I think she reasoned that if I'd thrown the ball away, I must not want it anymore, so she wouldn't bring it back.

That's the background to my experiment, which began with me sitting on the sofa and holding out my right hand such that my palm was up and my hand formed a soft cup. I rested my elbow on my knee so that I could keep my hand in place, at Lilly height, for as long as it took. The toy basket was on the floor, to the left of the sofa from where I sat, and the orange-and-white ball was sitting near the top, amongst her various other toys.

Miss Lilly, ever interested in what I was doing, was sitting on the floor in front of me. I imagined her going to the toy basket, selecting that particular ball from everything else that was in the basket, and then bringing it over and placing it in my outstretched hand.

Can you imagine what happened next?

Nothing. She just sat there, looking at me expectantly. Undeterred, I kept playing my little 'mental movie' of what I would like her to do, with no particular thought in mind other than "Wouldn't it be fun if Miss Lilly went to the basket, got that ball, and put it in my hand."

After a minute or so (although it felt like *hours*), Miss Lilly got bored and walked away. I got discouraged and stopped for a bit. Then I figured that I had nothing better to do, and I would really like to crack this nut, so I began again.

Miss Lilly came back and stood in front of me again, but this time she was watching me intently. I just kept running my mental movie, with no particular urgency or need for anything to happen; I simply thought it would be wonderful if she acted out my mental movie.

After what felt like an eternity, but which was probably only another minute, Miss Lilly went to the toy basket, picked up that particular ball, and then walked over and put it in my hand, with a "Well, that was too easy; what's next?" expression on her face.

I don't remember what we did next. I'm sure I made a big fuss of her 'cleverness', which would have baffled her no end. Such a simple thing to be praised for doing!

Many years have gone by since that day, and my mind is still blown by the result of that little experiment. I haven't dared to replicate it — no doubt, for fear of failing! But ever since that day I have tried to remember to play little mental movies whenever I'm with animals. I show them what I'm planning to do or what I'd like us to do together, and I explain *why* whenever it would make sense to do that.

For example, I'd show Miss Lilly a little movie of us getting in the car and going to our friends' (Kim and Walter's) place. She never liked travelling in the car, but she loved our friends and running wild on their farm with their dogs, so she was more enthusiastic about getting in the car when I would show her where we were going and what we'd be doing there.

In my next Miss Lilly story, I'll talk about the tyranny of time when operating in this way...

Miss Lilly takes her time

Time is something that has tyrannized me for pretty much my whole life. "Hurry up!" "Wait!" "Don't be late!" As a result, I hate to keep people waiting, and I hate to be kept waiting.

Miss Lilly didn't bother with all that nonsense. She could move with lightning speed when she wanted; but she was just as good at going slow, or not moving at all.

On our walks, I would usually go too quickly for her and I'd get impatient when she'd want to take her time and sniff every square inch of the way, veer off down a different trail, or 'go bush'. And heaven help us if we happened upon a site where another dog had peed! We'd be there for hours (or so it felt to me).

Most maddening was when she'd stand at the back door, deciding whether she wanted to be inside or outside... She loved to be outside, but she hated to get rained on. That was quite the dilemma when we lived in the Seattle area, where it rained for nine months of the year and dripped off the trees for the rest.

I'd long been of the view that I should be giving her as much freedom and choice in her daily life as I could manage under the circumstances. As we had a fully fenced yard, she had the choice of being inside or outside, whichever she pleased. She knew both words, so I would routinely ask her whether she wanted to be inside or outside. We didn't have a dog door, though, so she couldn't just come and go as she pleased; I had to be 'on the door'.

On several occasions, I found myself standing at the back door, holding it open for her as the chilly, wet wind blew in, impatient for her to make up her mind. I could see her weighing her options, because she would look in at the kitchen and then out again at the rain. Her eyebrows would lift and her ears would twitch as she looked at the rain, as if she was thinking "Maybe it'll stop soon." Our house was cozy and warm, but outside was vastly more interesting than inside.

Then it finally struck me: she was indeed considering her options, but unlike me, who was entrained to the immediate responses (and *expectations* of immediate response) of human communications, she was making her choice as though she had all the time in the world.

No, scratch that; as if time didn't exist. Because for her, human time *didn't* exist. *Dog* time did, and in dog time there are only a handful of times: meal time, play time, walk time, nap time, bed time, and getting out of bed time.

Over the years, Miss Lilly taught me by splendid example the importance of letting my watch battery go flat and ignoring the clock on the wall, and instead eating when I'm hungry, stopping when I'm full, resting when I'm tired, going to bed when I'm done for the day, getting up when I wake up, and so on.

I've been without the live-stream of *Miss Lilly's Lessons on Life* for over five years now, and I must admit that I've backslid a bit. (Miss Lilly completed her mission in 2017, at somewhere between 16 and 17 years of age.) Remembering how she'd take her time with important decisions such as inside or outside has gotten me thinking about time, and how I've been rushing headlong through life toward some ill-defined goal, when what I should be doing is slowing down and smelling all the great smells and exploring all the interesting things one finds along the way when we just *slow down*.

The curious thing is that magic happens — for example, inspiration lights on my mind like a butterfly on my shoulder — when I switch from human time to dog time...

Pollyanna and the art of seeing the whole picture

Have you ever been accused of being "a Pollyanna"? As in, "Oh, don't be a Pollyanna!" Or "You're such a Pollyanna!"

Or worse, have you ever heard yourself say, "I don't want to be a Pollyanna, but..."

OK, so the young Hayley Mills' depiction of Pollyanna makes me want to slap the girl, but that ungracious impulse aside, I want to make the case *for* being a Pollyanna.

It's clear to me that anyone who has a negative view of Pollyanna (and being "a Pollyanna" — Pollyanna-ism; yes, that's now a word!) has never read the book or seen a faithful (*i.e.,* unsentimental) screen adaptation of the story. Because if they had, then they'd know what it was really about:

The Glad Game.

Before he died, making her an orphan, Pollyanna's father taught her the Glad game, which basically goes like this:

Anytime something bad happens, say to yourself, "Even though [this bad thing] has happened, I'm glad that..." and then start naming some things you're glad about.

Before long, you're starting to feel a bit better, and you start to get some perspective — and you start to see solutions that might not have even occurred to you in your 'pre-glad' state.

In other words, the Glad game is an acknowledgement that, yes, a bad thing has happened, and it may even be awful; but good things are happening, too — all at the same time.

The Glad game is about practicing the art of seeing the whole picture. It's also about where you place your focus: on just the bad thing that's happened or on the whole picture, including all the good things, which usually far outnumber the bad.

When you start playing the Glad game with animals, funny things happen...

Whether it be a physical problem or a behavioral issue, it's remarkable what happens when you start naming some things that are going right: you start to see more things that are going right. And when you start looking for the improvements that you want to see, you start to see them.

For example, when you start (gently and inquisitively) looking for good behavior in an animal who's been behaving badly (according to our preferences, at least), the animal starts behaving better. (The key here is gentle and inquisitive attention or curiosity; as the Buddhists would say, 'nonattachment' to any particular outcome.)

Perhaps the behavior is just a little bit better at first, but if you keep looking for good behavior, and keep rewarding the little bit that you see, the animal offers more and more of the behavior you want, and less and less of the behavior you don't want.

Is this merely an example of reward-based training or is the animal actively participating in improving the relationship between us?

Are we making things happen or simply noticing that they've already happened, that they were already there?

Perhaps it's both.

The seeds of change were always there, but they may have needed a little encouragement to germinate and grow.

Either way, the change starts with us.

And it starts with us choosing to see the whole picture, rather than focusing just on what's wrong.

~ the end ~
(for now)

About the author

Christine (Chris) King is a holistic equine veterinarian who currently lives in southern Victoria (Australia). Her interests include the medical sciences (veterinary and human), complementary and alternative medicine, music, organic gardening, sustainable agriculture, nutrition, communication, spirituality, and the bonds we share with our animals.

Better Together is her tenth book.

Other books by Christine King

Equine Lameness (Equine Research Inc., 1997)

Preventing Colic in Horses (Paper Horse, 1999)

Preventing Laminitis in Horses (Paper Horse, 2000)

The Anima Herbal Recipe Book (Anima Books, 2011)

Nothing More is Needed (Anima Books, 2011)

Feeding Miss Lilly (Anima Books, 2014; revised 2022)

Retreat (Anima Books, 2022)

The Highly Sensitive Dog (Anima Books, 2022)

Stay connected at
animabooks.com.au